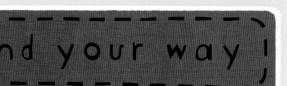

find your way
UNDER THE SEA

Paul Boston

QED

YOUR MISSION

Welcome to Merp Town. We need your help to finish building our castle. Find your way there by choosing which exits or entrances to follow on each page.

1
Choose your transport

Submarine

Sea Turtle

Seahorse

2
Trace a route

There are lots to choose from and you can go **BACKWARDS** and **FORWARDS** along the same road.

3
Collect on every page

Choose ONE of the missions below to help the Merps. You will find one of each object in every scene.

Collect 12 SHINY PEARLS to decorate the princess's bedroom.

Collect 12 BURGERS for the hungry castle builders.

Collect 12 SHARK TEETH to use as tools to help build the castle.

4 Use the book
LIKE A REAL MAP
Turn the pages and use co-ordinates in this book just like you would with a real map. You can find out more about co-ordinates on pages 4 and 5.

5 Solve maths puzzles
Along the way you will come across Merps who are lost or need your help. You will have to use your super maths skills to help them. You might be asked to count up to ten or to find a shape.

Welcome to Merp Town

Look at the map of Merp Town. Can you see where the castle is? That's where you need to get to. Let's use co-ordinates to help us describe where the castle is on the map.

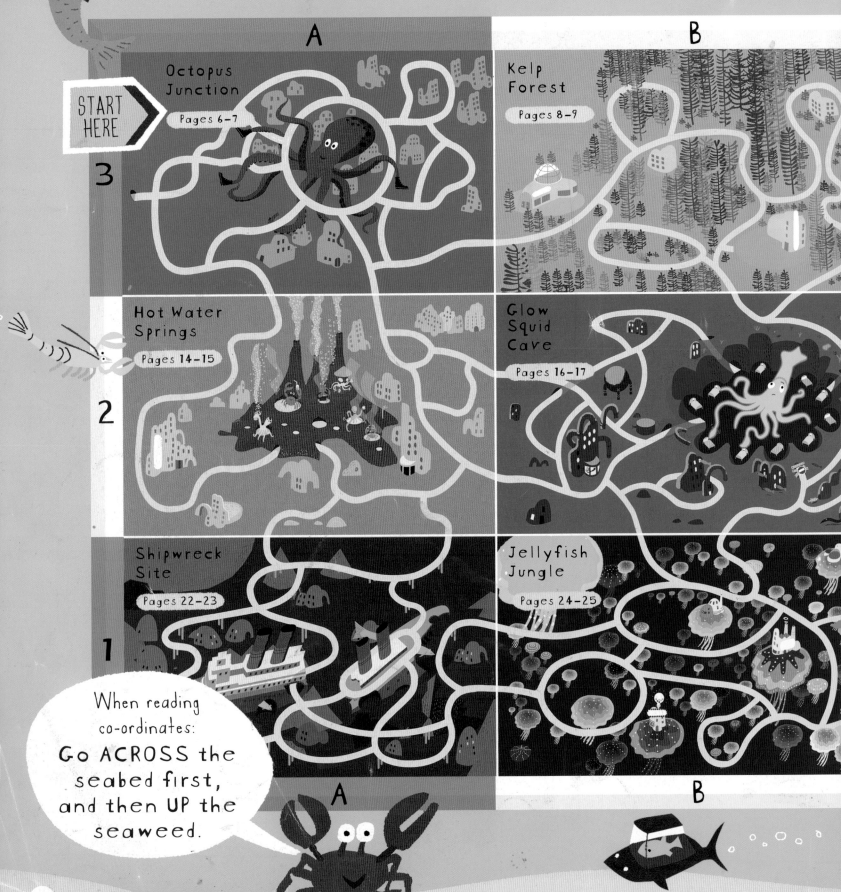

A

B

3

Octopus
Junction
Pages 6-7

START HERE

Kelp
Forest
Pages 8-9

2

Hot Water
Springs
Pages 14-15

Glow
Squid
Cave
Pages 16-17

1

Shipwreck
Site
Pages 22-23

Jellyfish
Jungle
Pages 24-25

When reading co-ordinates:
Go ACROSS the seabed first, and then UP the seaweed.

A

B

What are co-ordinates?

Co-ordinates are a set of letters and numbers that show where something is on a map. The letter comes first, followed by the number, so the castle is in **(D,1)**. Look for the co-ordinate symbol throughout the book.

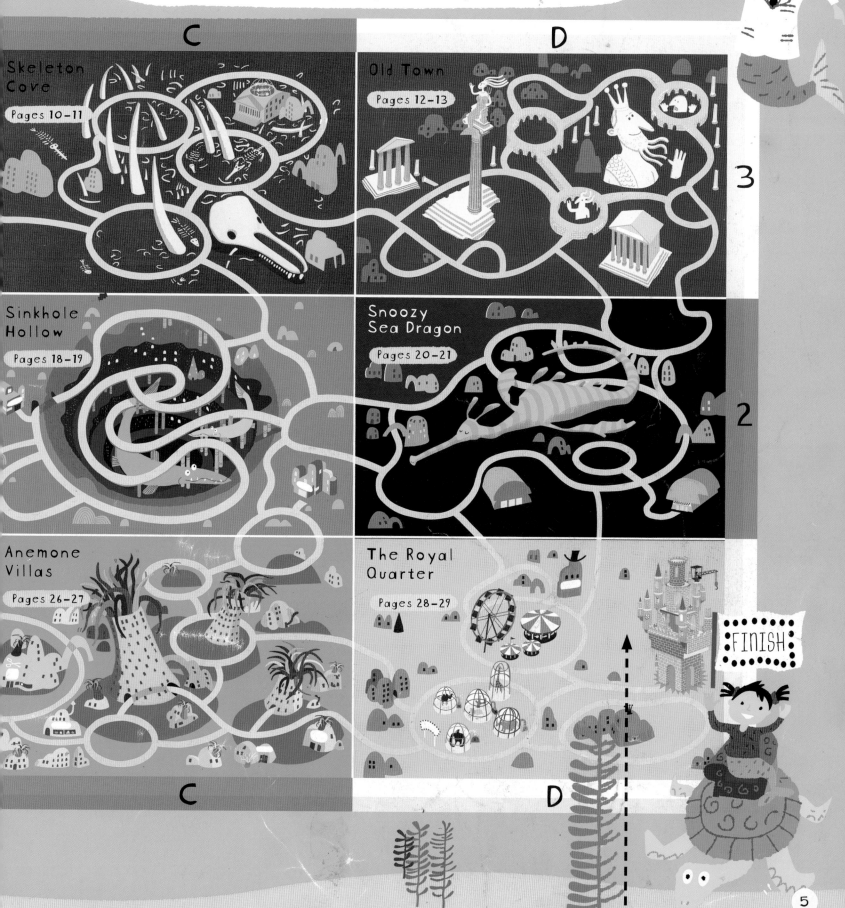

C

D

Skeleton Cove

Pages 10-11

Old Town

Pages 12-13

3

Sinkhole Hollow

Pages 18-19

Snoozy Sea Dragon

Pages 20-21

2

Anemone Villas

Pages 26-27

The Royal Quarter

Pages 28-29

FINISH

C

D

Oh no! Mr Tentacles is blocking the way! Find a way around him to carry on with your mission. Use your finger to help. Can you spot your object anywhere?

SHARK TOOTH

BURGER

PEARL

I'm lost! Can you please tell me the co-ordinates for the bank?

START HERE

Stop! Count how many shoes Mr Tentacles is missing before I let you pass.

OCTOPUS JUNCTION

AQUA PETS

Go to page 14

HOT WATER SPRINGS

A   B   C

3

2

1

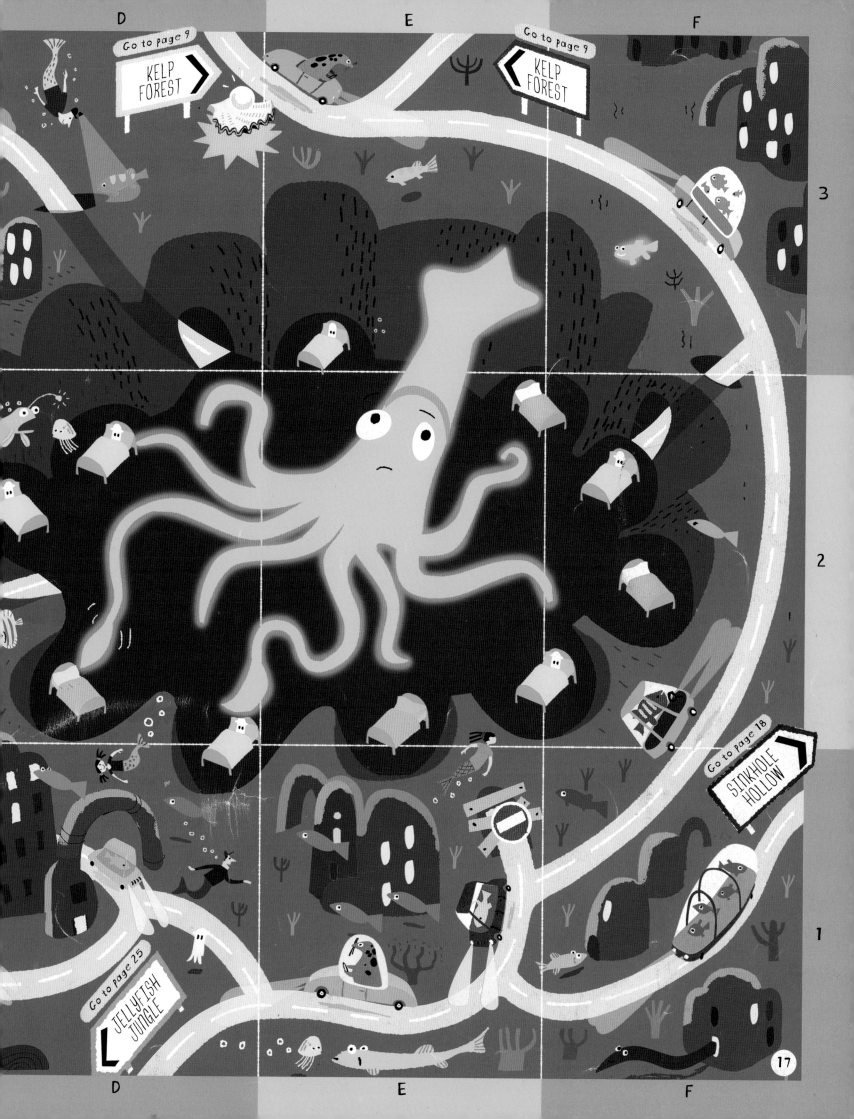

Go to page 9
KELP FOREST

Go to page 9
KELP FOREST

Go to page 18
SINKHOLE HOLLOW

Go to page 25
JELLYFISH JUNGLE

Welcome to the Shipwreck Site!

This old ruin was once a ship, which crashed and sunk to the bottom of the sea. It is too big to move, so the Merps have cleverly made tunnels through it.

SHARK TOOTH

BURGER

PEARL

Go to page 14

HOT WATER SPRINGS

⊙ Where is the treasure chest? I'm going to be rich! Yippee!

You have reached Anemone Villas!

Lots of Merps live here. Be careful not to get too close to the tentacles as you look for your object as they can sting!

SHARK TOOTH

BURGER

PEARL

Go to page 25

JELLYFISH JUNGLE

Hair Cuts

Which anemone building is the biggest?

Go to page 25

JELLYFISH JUNGLE

Bakery

ANEMONE VILLAS

Congratulations! You've made it to The Royal Quarter. Collect your object and head over to the castle. Be polite to the king and queen who live there!

SHARK TOOTH

BURGER

PEARL

Go to page 20
SNOOZY SEA DRAGON

Go to page 27
ANEMONE VILLAS

THE ROYAL QUARTER

Go to page 27
ANEMONE VILLAS

Which sea creature is winning the race?

Merp Games

28

MORE FUN UNDER THE SEA!

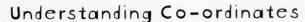

Understanding Co-ordinates

Encourage your child to look at other places where they might find co-ordinates, such as on an A-Z map. Draw a pirate's map together and plan your route to the treasure, or play a game of Battleships.

Counting

Go back through the book and look for more opportunities to encourage counting under the sea. How many arms does an octopus have? How many claws does a crab have?

Telling the Time

Make a simple clock with your child to encourage them to look closely at telling the time. Use a paper plate, and attach arms using a split pin or pipe cleaners. You could even decorate it to look like a turtle. Fill in the clock face using coloured pens. To go a step further, make paper 'flaps' which can be lifted up to reveal the minutes.

Recognising Shapes

Make a sea monster! Cut out lots of different 2D shapes from coloured paper. You could use triangles for the flippers, a circle for the body and squares for its scales. What shape would its teeth be? You could even try using 3D shapes from plasticine.

Maths Problems and Vocabulary

Go back through the book and look for opportunities to build on mathematic vocabulary and problem solving skills. For example, what is the total number of baby squid? Or, if there are three jellyfish with ten legs each, how many legs are there altogether?

Measurements

Using building blocks, make a little underwater town with your child. Can you make a really tall block of flats like the Anemone Villas? What about a long boat or a short submarine?

Quarto is the authority on a wide range of topics.

Quarto educates, entertains and enriches the lives of our readers—enthusiasts and lovers of hands-on living.

www.quartoknows.com

Written and edited by: Joanna McInerney and the QED team
Designed by: Mike Henson
Consultant: Alistair Bryce-Clegg

Copyright © QED Publishing 2016

First published in the UK in 2016 by QED Publishing
Part of The Quarto Group
The Old Brewery, 6 Blundell Street,
London, N7 9BH

A catalogue record for this book is available from the British Library.

ISBN 978 1 78493 632 7

Printed in China

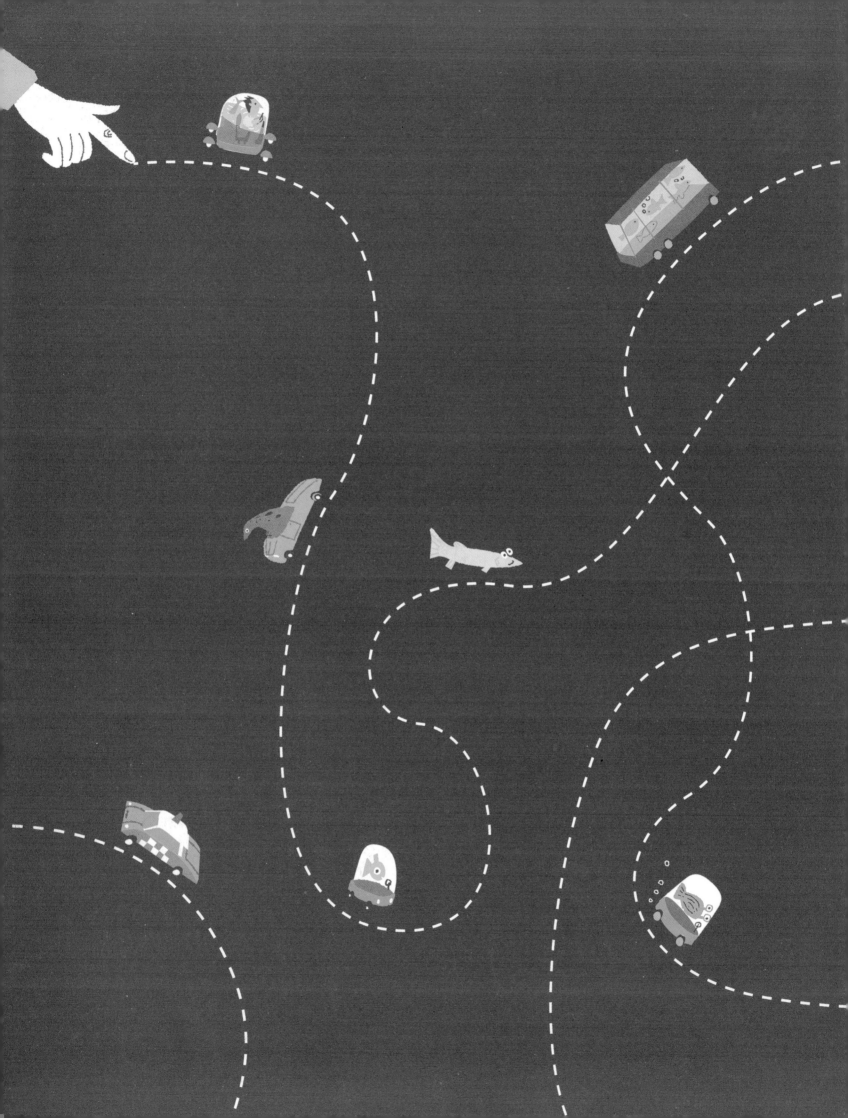